Across the HORIZON

stephanie d. moore

Jabez cried out to the God of Israel,
"Oh, that you would bless me and enlarge my territory!
Let your hand be with me, and keep me from harm so that I
will be free from pain." And God granted his request.

I Chronicles 4:10

Copyright © 2025 by Stephanie D. Moore

Published by
Moore Marketing and Communications, LLC

Kansas City, Missouri
StephanieDMoore.com
MooretoRead.com

In accordance with the U.S. Copyright Act of 1976, scanning, uploading, or electronic sharing of any part of this book, audio, written, or e-published is strictly prohibited and unlawful. No part of this book may be reproduced in any form by any means, including photocopying, electronic, mechanical, recording, or by any information storage and retrieval systems without permission in writing by the copyright owner.

Bulk copies or group sales of this book are available by contacting
Stephanie D. Moore at moore@stephaniedmoore.com or (405) 306-9833.

Moore, Stephanie D.
Across the Horizon: A 31-Day Devotional on Legacy Prayer

First Edition Printed July 2025
Printed in the USA.

Cover Design and Layout Design by
Moore Marketing and Communications, LLC.
All Rights Reserved.

Cover Photo used in design is an image generated using Adobe Firefly.

ISBN: 978-1-955544-43-6

*Jabez was more honorable than his brothers.
His mother had named him Jabez, saying, "I gave birth to him in pain." Jabez cried out to the God of Israel, "Oh, that you would bless me and enlarge my territory! Let your hand be with me, and keep me from harm so that I will be free from pain." And God granted his request.*

I Chronicles 4:9-10

Across the HORIZON

Introduction		9
Day 1	Humility	15
Day 2	Obedience in the Face of Adversity	19
Day 3	Allies	23
Day 4	On Display	25
Day 5	Rely Solely on God	27
Day 6	Ready for War	29
Day 7	New	31
Day 8	Dynasty	33
Day 9	Faith Over Fear	35
Day 10	Freedom	37
Day 11	Walk in the Light	39
Day 12	For His Glory	43
Day 13	Heavenly Defense	45
Day 14	A Life Without Fear	47
Day 15	Omnipresent God	51
Day 16	Caught in the Act	53
Day 17	Know that You Know	55
Day 18	Rest from War	57
Day 19	Never Our Battle	59
Day 20	A Resurrected Life	61
Day 21	The Vengeance of the Lord	63
Day 22	One with God	67
Day 23	A New Beginning	69
Day 24	Elevation	71
Day 25	It Won't Cost You Anything	73
Day 26	The Burden of the Prophet	75
Day 27	The Spirit of the Lord	77
Day 28	The Blessing of Wisdom	79
Day 29	Peace	81
Day 30	On the Mountaintop	83
Day 31	Beyond!	87

In Loving Memory

Allan "Grip" Smith

We always triumph through Christ

when people witness the effect

of the knowledge of Christ in our lives

everywhere we go.

2 Corinthians 2:14

Introduction

How we imagine our future matters to us and Jesus. What we hope for should be communicated to God, regularly, that he may guide us to our destination. Horizon Prayers are prayers that have the sole purpose of helping us to become all that God has created us to be.

One of my simplest Horizon prayers is the prayer of Jabez, "Lord, Bless me indeed," found in I Chronicles 4.

Horizon Prayers get down to the nitty gritty of what we hope for, they challenge our faith to believe that God is going to grant us our highest hopes, we just need to ask and believe that we can achieve them.

There is a remarkable difference between a lifestyle of daily prayer (to pray without ceasing) and intentional horizon prayers (prayers tied to your purpose, destiny, and legacy). Horizon prayers require research, soul searching, and intimacy with God.

mooretoread.com

Daily Prayer

Most Gracious and Heavenly Father,

We give you praise. We thank you for this moment to reflect, listen and share with an all-knowing, omnipresent, and benevolent God who loves us unconditionally.

Unless the Lord builds the house, those who build it labor in vain. Unless the Lord watches over the city, the watchman stays awake in vain. It is in vain that we rise up early and go late to rest, eating the bread of anxious toil; for he gives to his beloved sleep. (Psalm 127:1-2)

As we bring the seeds that only the Holy Spirit could have planted into our hearts, we pray that you guide us, speak to us, and protect not only the vision but the application of what you have defined as our purpose. However, our ability to walk in such great purpose, must first be preconditioned with prayer for forgiveness, mercy, and grace to do what God has called us to do. As Ezra and Nehemiah prayed as they conditioned themselves and the people of God to rebuild what was lost, we must also pray.

We are too ashamed and disgraced, our God, to lift up our faces to you, because our sins are higher than our heads and our guilt has reached to the heavens. From the days of our ancestors until now, our guilt has been great. Because of our sins, we and our kings and our priests have been subjected to the sword and captivity, to pillage and humiliation at the hand of foreign kings, as it is today.

But now, for a brief moment, the Lord our God has been gracious in leaving us a remnant and giving us a firm place in his sanctuary, and so our God gives light to our eyes and a little relief in our bondage. Though we are downtrodden, our God has not forsaken us in our detriment. He has shown us kindness: He has

granted us new life to rebuild the house of our God and repair its ruins, and he has given us a wall of protection. (Ezra 9:6-9)

Lord, the God of heaven, the great and awesome God, who keeps his covenant of love with those who love him and keep his commandments, let your ear be attentive and your eyes open to hear the prayer your servant is praying before you day and night for your servants, those saved by the sacrifice of Jesus Christ. We confess our sins, including myself and my father's family, have committed against you. We have acted very wickedly toward you. We have not obeyed the commands, decrees and laws you gave your servant Moses. Remember the instruction you gave your servant Moses, saying, 'If you are unfaithful, I will scatter you among the nations, but if you return to me and obey my commands, then even if your exiled people are at the farthest horizon, I will gather them from there and bring them to the place I have chosen as a dwelling for my Name. We are your servants and your people, whom you redeemed by your great strength and your mighty hand. Lord, let your ear be attentive to the prayer of this your servants and to the prayer of your servants who delight in revering your name. Give your servants success today by granting us favor in the presence of man. (Nehemiah 1: 5-11)

Lord as we seek you vertically each day to direct our path, we also pray horizontally that we might understand but a fractional resemblance of your intention for us. Just as Christ knew at an early age that he must be about his father's business, teach us to be about your business, purpose, and plan for our lives.

Surround us with those who can impact our destiny in magnificent ways. Open doors that no man can shut. Speak life to circumstances that threaten death. Keep your angels of protection around us so that we may arrive safely at our destination. You are the author and the finisher of our faith, grant us supernatural favor and discernment that we may do and be all that you have called us to do and be.

Help us to speak that vision into existence and to call those things that are not as though they already were. Help us to walk as leaders among our families and children reflecting the goodness of the Lord. Help us to show that God is with us as we walk in dark valleys among the shadow

of death. Prepare a table before us in the presence of our enemies, go before us and make every crooked place straight. And Lord, please help us to choose what is pleasing and profitable to bring about your purpose that we might sit at the table of conquerors in the beautiful by and by.

Lord, our goal is to hear you say,
"Well done, good and faithful servant."

In Jesus' Name, Amen

Humility

"Now, Lord my God, you have made your servant king in place of my father David. But I am only a little child and do not know how to carry out my duties. Your servant is here among the people you have chosen, a great people, too numerous to count or number. So give your servant a discerning heart to govern your people and to distinguish between right and wrong. For who is able to govern this great people of yours?"

I Kings 3:7

For many, the act of being humble seems unnecessary, but to be humble is to be sober-minded.

We are more fragile than we often think. Years of security (albeit financial, physical, emotional, or spiritual) can give us the impression that our areas of security are impenetrable or unbreakable.

Horizon prayer requires that we understand and embrace our vulnerability in such a way that we value prioritizing God. This means we worship him from our hearts, and that we are not using a system of worship that simply checks the boxes (church, tithe, study, pray, etc.), but to go deeper and develop a real relationship with Him.

Only then will we desire God more than any vain addition to our lives. In humility, we thank God for his protection, we praise God for his unconditional love, we ask God for help, we apologize to God

when we lose our way, we love others in the same way that God loves us, and we share God with as many as we can find.

This sense of humility often shows up in our daily 'guide my footsteps' prayers but how can it manifest in our across the horizon prayers?

> Therefore, with minds that are alert and fully sober, set your hope on the grace to be brought to you when Jesus Christ is revealed at his coming. (I Peter 1:13)

One way we can pray with destiny in mind is to understand that our existence is to serve God and introduce God to others. For some, this may seem like a heavy lift or even altogether unreasonable but God is, and we are because He is. If others that came before us had not taken the same mantle that God asks of us, we would not know him or the beautiful life he affords us.

King Solomon, in his humility, understood that he needed God, so he asked God to help him in a way that impacted his destiny in profound ways.

> When all Israel heard the verdict the king had given, they held the king in awe, because they saw that he had wisdom from God to administer justice. (I Kings 3:28)

Horizon prayer asks us to identify areas in our lives that we have elected to take the lead (as opposed to asking God for guidance), recognize how this skillset or area of our lives can be dramatically impacted and influence our destiny and purpose. We must ask God to show us the way to manage this area with excellence and how to recognize when we are walking in alignment with his will.

Releasing this area of our lives to God will not only give us peace, but will also help us to develop a foundation of understanding that can grow into other areas of our lives.

Obedience in the Face of Adversity

But Joseph said to them, "Don't be afraid. Am I in the place of God? You intended to harm me, but God intended it for good to accomplish what is now being done, the saving of many lives. So then, don't be afraid. I will provide for you and your children." And he reassured them and spoke kindly to them.

Genesis 50:19-21

Our purpose can be emotionally challenging at times. God's ways are not our ways. The Lord asks us to share his abundant and unconditional love with everyone, including those who are rude, unappreciative, and even evil at times. Despite what we experience or how we feel, God's goal doesn't change. He is the same, yesterday, today, and tomorrow - God is love.

When we pray daily for the Lord to guide our footsteps, we are asking for help in that moment, to overcome the daily challenge of meeting his request.

But when we pray horizontally, we are asking the Lord to change, in the long term, how we perceive emotionally challenging situations. This is a heart work that takes time that will undoubtedly

catapult us into our purpose-driven life. People we meet who exemplify God's love no matter how they are treated, are those who have walked with the Lord long enough to know that it is His desire that we let Him fight our battles. Our anger, sadness, or fear can subside when our greatest challenges are placed into God's hands.

Follow God's example, therefore, as dearly loved children and walk in the way of love, just as Christ loved us and gave himself up for us as a fragrant offering and sacrifice to God. (Ephesians 5:2)

In the same way, let your light shine before men, that they may see your good works, and glorify your Father which is in heaven. (Matthew 5:16)

Cast all your anxiety on him because he cares for you. Be alert and of a sober mind. Your enemy the devil prowls around like a roaring lion looking for someone to devour. Resist him, standing firm in the faith, because you know that the family of believers throughout the world is undergoing the same kind of sufferings. (I Peter 5:7-9)

In the Bible, Joseph son of Jacob, was violently thrown into a life of slavery, subjected to cruelty, and submitted to foreigners. This tumultuous, arduous, and painful life began with a prophecy, and his brother's jealousy. It all began when his brothers sold him into slavery, and many years later, without knowing what Joseph experienced because of their choices, they desperately needed his help. Joseph could have hurt them, but he didn't. Instead, he blessed them, protected them, and forgave them. You see, when Joseph experienced the hardships caused by his brothers, he walked with God and trusted God to see him through. Even when Joseph intentionally treated every person he encountered very well (giving them his all), he was still thrown into unfair situations, to the point of being falsely imprisoned. But then, just as suddenly as God allowed him to be subjected to slavery, he catapulted him into a place of distinction, authority, and wealth. When God allowed Joseph to rise it is because Joseph's life gave God the glory. The Lord positioned Joseph with the same power that those who mistreated him had, because God knew he would forgive, bless, and protect, when faced with those who caused him great pain.

As believers who have an intimate relationship with God we

understand how important it is that we obey His will, but it can often be much more difficult to walk it out. This is why embracing vertical (daily) and horizon (kingdom) prayer is critically important. We are his hands and his feet, but we cannot represent ourselves as such if we take the battle personally, it is never about us.

mooretoread.com

Allies

"Now then, please swear to me by the Lord that you will show kindness to my family, because I have shown kindness to you. Give me a sure sign that you will spare the lives of my father and mother, my brothers and sisters, and all who belong to them—and that you will save us from death."

"Our lives for your lives!" the men assured her. "If you don't tell what we are doing, we will treat you kindly and faithfully when the Lord gives us the land."

Joshua 2:12 - 14

When we dedicate our lives to Jesus Christ in gratitude of his love for us we learn to value the relationships we have with others, especially those that are beneficial to accomplish our purpose. I sincerely believe that God positions us to discover, witness, experience, and learn from those who have access to the tools and platforms our destiny requires.

However, we have a responsibility in the process of developing relationships to seek the knowledge we need to be successful. When we accept a position or role with a company, it will often come with a unique set of challenges, requests, and defined responsibilities. Through experience and exposure, we develop a greater

understanding on how specific services or products can be improved to serve clientele.

We seek God's assistance to not only help us to discern those that are good for us to be in relationship with but also to identify those who are toxic. We solicit God for help to broaden our horizon of understanding that we may see beyond our current circumstance to what can be. Then God will give us unique strategies to accomplish his goals and to bring about his purpose in our lives.

> Then Joshua son of Nun secretly sent two spies from Shittim. "Go, look over the land," he said, "especially Jericho." So they went and entered the house of a prostitute named Rahab and stayed there.
>
> Joshua 2:2

For the leader of the Israelites to seek assistance from a prostitute was unheard of, yet this was the best course for Joshua to gain insight, develop strategy, and to make an unexpected yet reliable ally.

At times, God will direct us to do what is seemingly unnatural, inappropriate, yet critical to accomplish our goals. In order to receive instruction that challenges our intelligence and understanding requires vertical and horizontal prayer to know who to trust and to do exactly as God tells us.

On Display

"Neither this man nor his parents sinned," said Jesus, "but this happened so that the works of God might be displayed in him.

John 9:3

    The world is full of judgmental people who measure others based on their own personal beliefs. But God has called each of us to be a light in the earth that reflects his character among men. It can seem easy for us to walk with our heads high and mighty when we know we are living a life that honors God, but what happens when our disabilities are on display?

    When our vulnerabilities are transparent for all to see, we are given a unique opportunity to shine a light before others. It is easy to embrace the attitude of a victim, or the anger of one oppressed, or perhaps to put on the mask as the great pretender… but when people are able to see us authentically go through some of the toughest moments of our lives we have a chance to show them how God impacts us personally despite our circumstance. We can show them how God gives us strength, how we depend on God to see us through, and how the joy that we have cannot be dimmed regardless of circumstance but remains because of our confidence in the one who lives within us.

When Jesus spit and mixed it with the dirt to make a mud that he could spread on the blind man's eyes it was a parable of God humbling himself to come to earth in the form of a man, that he might give each of us a part of himself by power of the Holy Spirit to bring healing to those who are blind and lost. This process of healing may begin with us but it is not supposed to end with us. We are to share this gift with others that they who are blind may also see and receive the healing that only God can give.

Life is not easy for anyone walking this earth.

Daily prayers allow us to survive our hardships day-by-day, but strategic prayers help us to embrace our vulnerabilities and allow them to empower us to bring God glory regardless of the circumstance. Like lessons before, this devotional is centered on using horizontal prayer to ask God to change the shape of our pot, as one does on the potter's wheel. For the drug addict, it is asking for God to remove the taste from their pallet, for the body riddled with cancer, it is for God to convert the pain to peace. No matter the circumstance, we replace the current impact of our vulnerability with our confidence and hope in God.

Some of the Pharisees said, "This man is not from God, for he does not keep the Sabbath." (John 9:16)

When God changes us, we do not look the same. Nor do we act the same. While our affliction was not given to us as a result of sin, our shift will reflect it is a result from being in the presence of God. This remarkable change in our lives is undeniable and will always point back to a miracle working God who loves us unconditionally.

This change can only occur with consistent prayer that is horizontally focused on redefining our structure that we might be well-suited for our God-given purpose.

Rely Solely on God

In that day the remnant of Israel, the survivors of Jacob, will no longer rely on him who struck them down but will truly rely on the Lord, the Holy One of Israel.

Isaiah 10:20

Our reliance on God reflects our trust in him and only him.

Do not put your trust in princes, in human beings, who cannot save. When their spirit departs, they return to the ground; on that very day their plans come to nothing. Blessed are those whose help is the God of Jacob, whose hope is in the Lord their God.

(Psalm 146:3-5)

There is no doubt that as believers we trust God emphatically. But it is difficult not to put faith in men that seem or appear to be faithful or at the very least reflect a fraction of loyalty to us. But therein lies the purpose of the resounding message - we cannot trust anyone but God.

The truth is no matter how well we think we know someone there are always things we simply do not know. When we learn to discern God's voice from that of our own and honor and esteem his

voice above our most trusted advisors, friends, and family - we are walking in alignment with the Holy Spirit.

For those who have not developed this type of trust in God alone and even for those who feel that they have, horizontal prayer and authentic worship are the catalysts to developing that trust. The devil can and will use anyone available to dissuade us from trusting the Word of God - he will even use those we love and admire most.

It is our responsibility to seek the power of the Holy Spirit to help us hear God clearly, and trust him only.

Ready for War

When Pharaoh let the people go, God did not lead them on the road through the Philistine country, though that was shorter. For God said, "If they face war, they might change their minds and return to Egypt." So God led the people around by the desert road toward the Red Sea. The Israelites went up out of Egypt ready for battle.

Exodus 13:17-18

    A battle is but a moment, but a war is ongoing and can seem endless for those involved. When we pray for our daily needs, we are preparing for the day, for God to go before us and to make every crooked place straight. We may pray for direction, correction, protection or provision. But when we pray horizontally, we are praying for the war, for our God-given purpose to be completed in the way God originally designed.

    Horizon prayers must be strategic. Joseph, a humble servant of God, who was despised and sold into slavery by his siblings fulfilled his purpose. He recognized as a young man that he was different. God gave him dreams of his future and he could see it far off. While in his day-to-day life, he wanted sorely to be accepted by his peers, he soon recognized that despite his circumstances, he was called to be greater. No matter how difficult, arduous, unfair, or hurtful - Joseph kept his mind, heart, and soul in alignment with God's will for his life.

     When the Israelites were freed from Egyptian slavery, they were ready for a battle but not a war. Like the Israelites, God is preparing us that we may not fall away or give up because a war can go on for years. It is not a battle. Therefore, when we pray we must arm and equip not only our physical state, but most importantly our spiritual state - because a war brings great loss and hardship, and casualties lost that no one may expect. A war changes the landscape and our view of what once was and also what we imagine may be. We recognize not only our vulnerabilities but also our strengths.

     When we pray horizontally, we are preparing for war through strategic prayer. We pray for the strength to endure, the discernment to see with the eyes of God, the heart to forgive those who continually abuse their power, and the ability to be and become all that God has called us to be.

New

God said to him, "Your name is Jacob, but you will no longer be called Jacob; your name will be Israel." So he named him Israel.

Genesis 35:10

Jacob was called to return to Bethel where he once had an intimate and profound conversation with God. He was called to build an altar of remembrance in that place. Shortly after, his life changed dramatically and his destiny was activated, cemented in time that we who have come after may look back and see how God used him to bless us.

If you know the backstory of Jacob, it may surprise you that he was the one selected to become the father of the twelve tribes of Israel. But the blessing, despite the twisted way in which it was received, fell upon him and his household and it was he whom God chose to walk and usher in such an important milestone for the people of God.

No matter our background, or our poor decisions, God can still use each of us to do his will if we are willing to walk with him according to his plan. On that evening in Bethel, as he dreamed, God revealed his destiny to him in a profound way. He knew who he was, what he had done, and the life he seemed destined to live if he were not to have the guidance, support, and protection of God.

That moment in Bethel with God was a horizontal prayer moment for Jacob.

Then Jacob made a vow, saying, "If God will be with me and will watch over me on this journey I am taking and will give me food to eat and clothes to wear so that I return safely to my father's household, then the Lord will be my God and this stone that I have set up as a pillar will be God's house, and of all that you give me I will give you a tenth."

Genesis 28:20-22

Our prayers to God have power. Our actions before God have meaning. God sees the intentions of our hearts and he prepares us for what is to come and what has been done. In the most critical moments of horizontal prayer, we are blessed to not only pray to God, but to also hear from God. We need to make sure we are paying attention that we may receive his instruction in our life's most pivotal moments.

Dynasty

Their father Ephraim mourned for them many days, and his relatives came to comfort him. Then he made love to his wife again, and she became pregnant and gave birth to a son. He named him Beriah, because there had been misfortune in his family.

I Chronicles 7:22-23

Ephraim and Manasseh were brothers. Their father, Joseph, was the second in command in Egypt, and scorned by his siblings in his youth. They grew up with money, power, and fame by way of relationship to their father.

Traditionally, the older brother would be blessed by the patriarch of the family, but when Joseph brought his sons to his father, his father chose to bless the younger brother, Ephraim.

Through the lineage of Ephraim, we see Joshua, the son of Nun, who helped the Israelites enter into the Promised Land. It is Ephraim's family that was blessed to receive the land of Bethel, where Jacob became Israel and received the revelation that he and his descendants would own that very land one day. Bethel is where Israel was instructed to build an altar to God in remembrance of God.

In contrast, we see that the lineage of his brother, Manasseh is

disconnected from the traditional ways of the family. The succession of descendants from Israel, father of Jacob, father of Joseph, father of Ephraim and Manasseh, are fighting men, some prepared for battle - others for war. Manasseh's children are simply named without much connection or declaration of their preparedness to serve in the hierarchical dynasty.

Likewise, a man who gains wealth can leave an inheritance for his children, but it is impossible to leave a blessing for those who come behind you without horizontal prayer to God. Material gain is superficial and topical, giving an outward appearance that man can see, but spiritual gain is deep like a great tree with a root system that spans generations. It is the remembrance that God saved us, loves us, and will care for us - if we trust him.

Know therefore that the Lord your God is God; he is the faithful God, keeping his covenant of love to a thousand generations of those who love him and keep his commandments. (Deuteronomy 7:9)

When we pray horizontally for our children and their children, we are entrusting God to manage a future we will not be a direct part of. We are expressing a desire for our children to have and appreciate the very relationship we have with our Father. In doing so, we pray for a succession of leaders who will influence the world with a heart led by our Heavenly Father rather than money, power, or fame.

Faith Over Fear

Do not be afraid of them; the Lord your God himself will fight for you.

Deuteronomy 3:22

Fear will cause us to become angry when anger is not necessary. Fear prevented Moses from entering the Promised Land and allowed Joshua to take the lead.

As ministers of the gospel, we must do our very best to exemplify the core characteristic of Christ in all matters. When Christ was mocked, he did not lash out in anger, even when he knew death was imminent. Instead, he forgave the very people he taught, healed and performed miracles before as they cried, "Crucify Him!"

This is not a characteristic we are born with, it is a characteristic we must intentionally develop. Moses is a great example of a servant of God, who spent an enormous amount of time with God and who was even referred to as a friend of God, yet could not control his anger.

Moses was often accused of trying to usurp a leadership position that he did not hold. In this, God himself defended him. Moses often pleaded with God to have mercy on the Israelites who chose sin over God, time after time. Yet despite God's defense, and

his relentless intercession for others, he had moments of weakness that resulted in angry outbursts. From the breaking of the God-stroked Ten Commandments to the striking of the rock to bring water for a thirsty and travel-worn group of Israelites, Moses had a hard time controlling his disruptive and un-Christlike outbursts.

This is a cautionary tale for those of us who walk with God in our hearts and minds. For if Moses, a man who spent endless amounts of time communing with God yet could not control his anger - what does it say about us?

Anger is rooted in fear. Moses feared the worst. He knew how the behavior of the Israelites made God feel (or at least how he interpreted God felt). Therefore, he at times, would embody the emotional weight of God's pain and express it with anger. But these actions could not go into the next leg of the journey, for anger may be useful in a battle, but it is of no use in a war. A war requires strategy and discipline to make and execute wise decisions in a timely manner.

Horizontal prayer is strategic, intentional, and considers tomorrow while living today. The only way we can overcome fear is by faith. Faith allows us to lose a battle without fear, knowing we will win the war. While all of the Israelites did not make it into the Promised Land, those that should, did. We want to make sure that we and our descendants, those that God has called us to serve and love, can all make it there as well. We must learn, pray, and practice faith over fear every day.

Freedom

But now, after that ye have known God, or rather are known of God, how turn ye again to the weak and beggarly elements, whereunto ye desire again to be in bondage?

Galatians 4:8

As Christians, we are very aware of the price Christ paid that we might obtain freedom from sin. But perhaps, we don't truly appreciate the value of being free from sin as much as we ought. Sin is pervasive, sneaky, and comes upon us at the most inopportune times. Sin is a bully - it is relentless and unforgiving.

The thief comes only to steal and kill and destroy; I have come that they may have life, and have it to the full. (John 10:10)

The value of freedom is an eternal life. On this earth, we see the finite attribute of death and how when one is gone from this world, they are truly no longer present with us. God promises us that we will be changed. We do not have a definition of what that change will be, we just know that the day we leave life on this earth, we are present with God.

A lifetime of choosing life over death requires trust, discipline, and an understanding of what you are fighting for. In it's simplicity it is like a new promotion, a new house, a budget, a diet, or saving for

retirement, or to buy a new car. You know what you want is afar, but you also know what you must to do achieve your goals. The greater your desire, the more likely you are to meet those goals.

Horizontal prayer asserts through humility, that we are weak but that Christ is strong. It asserts that we recognize in our own mind, body, and soul, fighting sin without spiritual tools is futile. We need Christ to help us to recognize sin afar off, but to also aide us in combatting a desire or taste for sin in our lives. We must ask God to replace that desire with the desire to love and serve him in humility and truth. God does not expect us to be perfect, that is why Christ died for us. What he does desire is that we love him with all of our heart, mind, body, and soul.

While most horizontal prayer we pray is for others and the kingdom, this part of horizontal prayer is selfishly for us. We need and desire the peace that comes with living a life that honors God in wholeness and truth.

Walk in the Light

Come, descendants of Jacob, let us walk in the light of the Lord.

Isaiah 2:5

When we are intentional about our lives, we plan everything. We know where we are going, how we plan to get there, and why it is important we accomplish our goals. But so often, when it comes to our spiritual destination, we lay caution to the wind, allowing anyone with an idea, reflection or thought to provide insight into what we believe. But God shares that man is not to be trusted. The only relationship we can truly rely on is our relationship with God.

When we have a desire, we know what is required. If our desire is God, the requirement is to know Him and to know that he recognizes us as his own. This indicates that we must know and understand what the Word teaches us and that we have a desire to walk in alignment with the will of God as described in His Word.

We act to ensure our goals are met. Our actions are indications to God of who we are, what is most important to us, and what we believe is our responsible action. Romans chapter twelve is a great reflection of a heart, mind, body and soul committed to walk in the light of God. It teaches us to present our bodies as a living sacrifice, as humble servants, and to love others fully.

Love must be sincere. Hate what is evil; cling to what is good. Be devoted to one another in love. Honor one another above yourselves. Never be lacking in zeal, but keep your spiritual fervor, serving the Lord. Be joyful in hope, patient in affliction, faithful in prayer. Share with the Lord's people who are in need. Practice hospitality.

Romans 12:9-13

When it is all said and done, our goal is to hear our Lord say, "Well done, good and faithful servant." But we are sinners, born in sin, and living in natural bodies that do not always want to walk in the will of God. Paul wrote it best in Romans chapter seven.

Now if I do what I do not want to do, it is no longer I who do it, but it is sin living in me that does it.

So I find this law at work: Although I want to do good, evil is right there with me. For in my inner being I delight in God's law; but I see another law at work in me, waging war against the law of my mind and making me a prisoner of the law of sin at work within me. What a wretched man I am! Who will rescue me from this body that is subject to death? Thanks be to God, who delivers me through Jesus Christ our Lord!

So then, I myself in my mind am a slave to God's law, but in my sinful nature a slave to the law of sin. (Romans 7:20 - 25)

To walk with intention, and to know the true state of your being is to acknowledge that we are weak and God is strong. No matter how good a man professes he is, he is always going to be a sinner saved by grace. Our goal is to balance what we believe with an acknowledgement of who we are. This is why having an authentic relationship with God is at the center of the our ability to walk in the light.

If we have an authentic relationship with God, we can admit to God all things for we know in our hearts he is omnipresent and all knowing so there is no need in ignoring the elephant in the room. Our

hearts must confess our weakness and desire to do things that are not in the will of God, while also thanking God for his unending mercy and grace. This is why Christ died for us, that we may understand the true nature of God, and his unending love for us.

But he said to me, "My grace is sufficient for you, for my power is made perfect in weakness." Therefore I will boast all the more gladly about my weaknesses, so that Christ's power may rest on me. (2 Corinthians 12:9)

When we pray horizontally, we pray that we not only understand and walk in the light of God, but that we are also able to articulate through word and action what a life with God looks like. We pray to become the "living proof" of God's love exemplified through us, in weakness and strength, but ultimately through living intentional lives. We pray horizontally, that our "light" may shine so that others may look and thank God for our example in their lives.

For His Glory

Jesus called his twelve disciples to him and gave them authority to drive out impure spirits and to heal every disease and sickness.

Matthew 10:1

The most beautiful moments in life are encased by authentic connection and understanding.

There are many people who feel trapped by their circumstances, such as single mothers who are struggling to juggle life, responsibility, and personal growth. Perhaps the aging person without enough retirement who suddenly realizes they are going to suffer a life of servitude or face destitute outcomes. Perhaps the parent of a child experiencing health issues that they cannot cure, or financially sustain…

As a disciple of Jesus Christ, there are many ways we can help others. We can pray, provide assistance, call, or give in the time of need. God has given each of us the power and authority to not only choose to take any of these actions, but to also elect who we provide this form of love to.

The opportunity to serve others in love are endless. When

we choose to do so as followers of Christ, we are sharing his love with those who may not know him. It gives us an opportunity to introduce Christ in a way that allows the recipient to know that God sees them, he loves them, and he cares for them.

However, when we choose to live a life of love, we will face opposition. Opposition can come in many forms and the goal of opposition is to stop us from choosing love over our personal ambitions, material gain, or power.

Horizontal prayer allows us to pray strategically to live a life that prioritizes kingdom over day-to-day struggles. Horizontal prayer aides in calling on the power of the Holy Spirit to guide us as we heal, help, and hold onto those that are lost, sick, and in need of our love. Loving others is a lifelong journey that allows God to get the glory. Not so that he can be glorious, but so that he is able to share his love with others as he has shared it with us.

The most beautiful moments in life are encased by authentic connection and understanding.

Heavenly Defense

All my enemies will be overwhelmed with shame and anguish; they will turn back and suddenly be put to shame.

Psalm 6:10

When I began the journey to write this book and the others God will assign this year, God told me to begin each day praying specifically and strategically. He told me to pray, in this order, Psalm 91, Psalm 35, and finally a prayer over my books. The prayer uniquely enough, I asked ChatGPT to write for me.

So for the last month or so, I have started my day with this unique prayer comprised of the above. In doing so, I wake up each day feeling confident that God has gone before me and that no matter what the day may bring, I am resting beneath the shadow of his wings. God has me covered.

For He shall give His angels charge over you, To keep you in all your ways. (Psalm 91:11)

This is the benefit of Horizontal prayer, it not only allows us to speak the Word of God consistently, activating the work of God's angels, but it also gives us personal peace and confidence knowing we have called on the Almighty to protect us. Beyond providing the peace we seek daily, we are praying for a lifestyle change - a covered

life.

> Whoever dwells in the shelter of the Most High will rest in the shadow of the Almighty. He will cover you with his feathers, and under his wings you will find refuge; his faithfulness will be your shield and rampart. (Psalm 91:1,4)

This lifestyle change, this prayer for God to shift our atmosphere replacing all ill will with His Will will prepare a table before us in the presence of our enemies. We don't have to wish ill upon those who hurt us. We don't need to desire the riches of our enemies. Instead, if we simply have faith, God will rain blessings upon us in the face of our opposition.

"...vengeance is mine, saith the Lord, I will repay," God has promised us, those who trust him, that not only will he protect us but he is also going to take vengeance on those who wronged us. This is our heavenly defense.

A Life Without Fear

The Lord said to Joshua, "Do not be afraid of them; I have given them into your hand. Not one of them will be able to withstand you."

Joshua 10:8

To imagine a life without fear is tough. Change is scary. There is all manner of circumstance that could justify being fearful. Health scares, financial insecurity, physical threat, and emotional unwellness make us uneasy and uncertain. So how do we even imagine living a life without fear?

God desires that we trust him with the innocence and ignorance of a small child. When we put our lives in this perspective, children don't actually know that they should fear something until they learn different. Exposure is everything. If we are ingesting the Word of God daily, spending intimate time with him, fellowshipping with others who worship, praying and giving him praise, that sudden and seemingly crazy circumstance is secondary to our first belief which is to trust God.

When our enemy comes in like a flood, God will rectify that situation all on his own. In all situations, we must turn it over to the Lord. This is a change in the way we perceive circumstance

and allows us to live a life of peace. This is a peace that surpasses all understanding because to the person on the outside looking in, we look surrounded - down for the count. But God. God is our source, not the gift giver, the supervisor, the landlord, the president, our spouse or our friends, only God.

When we give God our burdens, he orders our footsteps. He goes before us to make every crooked place straight. The goal of horizontal prayer is to acknowledge him first, not once when it comes to mind, but everytime we are burdened with the fallacies of life. In horizontal prayer, we are asking God to shift the way we perceive situations and to recall his sovereignty first, to acknowledge his superiority first, to believe he is in control, first. We must keep God first in all things. This is critical for us to walk though the fire unscathed like three Hebrew boys, or to let the water get up to our neck but not overtake us - this is how we make the sun stand still.

You see life is full of ups and downs, highs and lows, impracticality and practicality - but in all things we are to give thanks, for if it were allowed, we must acknowledge that it is the Will of God. All things are not good, but all things work together for the good.

In the Bible, Gibeon was a strong and well-respected community. When their neighbors saw that the Gibeonites, a community they respected, surrendered to the Israelites, they were struck with fear. Five kings banded together to attack Gibeon. They assumed in their collective strength, they could overcome the Israelites regardless of their belief in God. Gibeon called on the Israelites for help and the Israelites came to help them.

> The Lord said to Joshua, "Do not be afraid of them;
> I have given them into your hand. Not one of them
> will be able to withstand you." (Joshua 10:8)

God was right there, in the moment, he immediately assured Joshua that the Israelites would be victorious.

This is how God works when you trust him. You can speak to

the circumstance in your life, just like Jesus did when he told the wind to be still, and God will count it as prayer. We see this exemplified in Joshua chapter 10.

On the day the Lord gave the Amorites over to Israel, Joshua said to the Lord in the presence of Israel:

"Sun, stand still over Gibeon, and you, moon, over the Valley of Aijalon."

So the sun stood still, and the moon stopped, till the nation avenged itself on its enemies. (Joshua 10:12-13a)

Horizontal prayer helps us shift not only our perception, but also our actions in response to circumstances.

Omnipresent God

"Yet I will show love to Judah; and I will save them—not by bow, sword or battle, or by horses and horsemen, but I, the Lord their God, will save them."

Hosea 1:7

When Solomon, the Israelite king, sinned against God by marrying the forbidden women in other nations, and likewise allowing their religious traditions to rest in God's land, the children of God were split into two factions: the Israelites and Judaens.

Judah was the branch with only two tribes, Israel was made up of ten tribes. David's bloodline was in the Judean branch. God did this because he made a promise to King David that the Messiah would come from his bloodline and within David's succession their would always be a king unto God.

In the book of Hosea, chapter one, God draws a line of distinction between those who worship and those who choose not to worship. Daily prayer is a byproduct of consistent worship, but Horizontal prayer creates the framework by which we develop consistent worship.

Worship: prayer, praise, and spending intimate time with God,

reading the Word of God, and sharing the gospel with others through word and deed - are a sweet fragrance to God. He loves when we choose to place him first in our lives, in turn, God promises that he will care for us as well. He takes our defense personally.

God promises us that if we are consistent, making his worship a lifestyle (not only a cry to God in moments of distress or a glimmer of praise when things are extremely good), that he is not going to send anyone else to do the job, but he himself will come and see about us. This is evidenced when the cries of his people reached him and the triune God came to see what was going on.

> Then the Lord said, "The outcry against Sodom and Gomorrah is so great and their sin so grievous that I will go down and see if what they have done is as bad as the outcry that has reached me. If not, I will know." (Genesis 18:20-21)

> During that long period, the king of Egypt died. The Israelites groaned in their slavery and cried out, and their cry for help because of their slavery went up to God. God heard their groaning and he remembered his covenant with Abraham, with Isaac and with Jacob. So God looked on the Israelites and was concerned about them. (Exodus 2:23-25)

> "Go back and tell Hezekiah, the ruler of my people, 'This is what the Lord, the God of your father David, says: I have heard your prayer and seen your tears; I will heal you. On the third day from now you will go up to the temple of the Lord." (2 Kings 20:5)

When God sees that we are here for the long haul, not conveniently, as we learn as a child, simply going to church each Sunday, but fully committed, worshipping him morning, noon, and night, God sees us and he hears our cries.

Caught in the Act

The teachers of the law and the Pharisees brought in a woman caught in adultery. They made her stand before the group and said to Jesus, "Teacher, this woman was caught in the act of adultery. In the Law Moses commanded us to stone such women. Now what do you say?" They were using this question as a trap, in order to have a basis for accusing him.

John 8:3-6

We are all sinners and fall short of the glory of God. There is no question in that.

But Jesus wasn't a sinner. He did not harbor ill will toward anyone. But he could accurately measure the hearts of those with bad intentions. In the story of the woman caught in adultery, he knew that the public accusations to embarrass, shame and even kill the woman who was caught was simply so that they could in turn, accuse him.

We too will experience public shame, hurtful scenarios, and be accused of things we had no intention of doing - all in service to God. But the battle is not ours, it belongs to the Lord. Satan is the accuser of the brethren. This we must remember as we encounter unfair situations.

We have a heavenly defense from an omniscient, benevolent, and omnipresent God. We are resting beneath the shadow of his

wings, and we must remember that. This is why horizontal prayer that covers our lifestyle is so important. We must intentionally seek to be what God has called us to be that we may live purpose-driven lives.

In this way, we know, without a doubt, that God is for us. God sees our hearts, our intentions, and our ways. He knows everything about us. While the situation we may face may be embarrassing, purposely hurtful, or painful in a plethora of ways - God has not allowed us to suffer more than his son, Jesus did that we may have eternal life.

Keep praying, horizontally, for a lifestyle that renders us, "Caught in the Act" of doing the will of God.

Know that You Know

And he said unto them, This kind can come forth by nothing, but by prayer and fasting.

Mark 9:29

Our belief in God is not a benefit. Our faith is the foundation by which we make decisions that impact not only our lives but the lives of others. Our trust of God changes how we respond to adversity. Our internal compass directs how we consider the ramification of our choices before they become decisions.

Therefore, we are challenged with coordinating our behavior to our beliefs. We must move beyond our mental and spiritual knowledge to form a connection with our behaviors by shifting from intention to action.

Horizontal prayer makes this a reality. Across the horizon, we recognize that unexpected circumstances arise without warning. If we are not in a state of consistent and continual worship, we will not be prepared for these unexpected circumstances.

This is best illustrated in Mark, chapter nine, which shares that Jesus came upon his disciples surrounded by religious leaders. Jesus could hear a great argument and at the heart of it was a troubled father whose son seemingly suffered from the possession of a demon.

This possession was similar in state to epileptic attacks that many suffer today, causing the son to be placed in dangerous situations that could take his life.

Jesus spoke to the father of the child and recognized the young man's father had doubt in Jesus' ability to heal his child. Jesus told him, quite sternly, his child's healing could only come if he believed.

Moments later, the demon came out of the young man and Jesus was helping him to his feet.

When Jesus and his disciples were alone some time after the event, he was asked by his disciples why they were unable to release the demon themselves. Jesus informed them that some possessions could only come forth by prayer and fasting.

This is the point of belief. When you believe in God, you develop a way of worship. We see often in scripture that Jesus went alone to pray. He spent intimate time with God on a regular basis. He must have also practiced the act of fasting on a regular basis as when he 'stumbled upon' this incident, he was adequately prepared to act - not only based on his belief, but also based upon his lifestyle of worship.

Horizontal prayer helps us to place our actions in alignment with our beliefs. In doing so, we are adequately prepared to handle life's toughest situations with God at the center, our faith on assignment, as our worship testifies on our behalf.

Anyone watching us can recognize that 'we know that we know' God is for us and that no weapon formed will be successful against us.

Rest from War

So Joshua took the whole land, according to all that the Lord said unto Moses; and Joshua gave it for an inheritance unto Israel according to their divisions by their tribes. And the land rested from war.

Joshua 11:23

Without Jesus the people of the earth were unsafe from eternal damnation and death. Jesus had to come clothed in the full armor of God that he might save us from our sins. In doing so, he has provided us rest from the eternal war. This does not mean we will not face battles, what it means is that God will see us through each that we may not walk alone.

Truth is nowhere to be found, and whoever shuns evil becomes a prey. The Lord looked and was displeased that there was no justice. He saw that there was no one, he was appalled that there was no one to intervene; so his own arm achieved salvation for him, and his own righteousness sustained him.

He put on righteousness as his breastplate, and the helmet of salvation on his head; he put on the garments of vengeance and wrapped himself in zeal as in a cloak. According to what

they have done, so will he repay wrath to his enemies and retribution to his foes; he will repay the islands their due.

From the west, people will fear the name of the Lord, and from the rising of the sun, they will revere his glory. For he will come like a pent-up flood that the breath of the Lord drives along. (Isaiah 59:15-19)

Horizontal prayer acknowledges that God is in control, that it is Jesus Christ who has saved us from our sins, not we ourselves. Horizontal prayer is a lifelong prayer of forgiveness and a quest for guidance that we man not only show up as our "best" selves but that we also reflect the love of Christ in all that we say and do.

Across the horizon of our lives, we will need and extend forgiveness. Like Joshua in chapter 11, we will need the guidance of God as we embark on wars we did not wage, fight battles we did not brew, and defend those who would not defend us. We must pray to be clothed in the full armor of God each day, not just today but in every tomorrow.

Horizontal prayer not only clothes us in our rightful garments of praise, gratitude, humility and grace, but it also provides a peace that surpasses understanding and a confidence that rests solely upon the shoulders of God. For if God be for us, who possibly could be against us?

Never Our Battle

Jephthah answered, "I and my people were engaged in a great struggle with the Ammonites, and although I called, you didn't save me out of their hands. When I saw that you wouldn't help, I took my life in my hands and crossed over to fight the Ammonites, and the Lord gave me the victory over them. Now why have you come up today to fight me?"

Judges 12:2-3

There are enemies who pursue us only because we are children of the Most High God. We can always recognize these battles because despite our best efforts, God will ensure we are solely dependent on Him alone. God is enough.

Horizontal prayer allows us to distinguish a couple of tale-tell signs in spiritual warfare. For one, horizontal prayer opens our eyes to see our enemies clearly - granting us a level of discernment we would not have recognized without the favor of God.

Secondly, it will give you a confidence that only God can provide. When we hear God say, "Yes," we know that we are safe in his hands. This can only come from having a consistent prayer life and having the ability to recognize God's voice. When God directs us, no matter how scary it may seem, we know that we are in good

hands.

Thirdly, we can know that no matter the outcome, it is the will of God. Our battles are not our battles, we are simply the tool that God uses to execute his will in the earth. Horizontal prayer helps us to clearly identify how we are operating within the body of Christ and that our God is a strategic God. Some things must occur that others may then fall in alignment.

Finally, God is always for us. He desires that we live a life that brings him honor and glory. Our ways are not God's ways. Therefore, in moments of battle, fights we did not start, we can know that God is going to direct us in a way that not only allows us to receive the victory but that also brings glory to his name. In the end, our responsibility is to let our light shine, that men may glorify our Father in heaven.

A Resurrected Life

"It is when a person walks at night that they stumble, for they have no light."

John 11:10

When I was a young woman, I saw the most influential person in my life, laying in a coffin. It was painfully obvious to me that he was no longer there. He was gone, and my last goodbye was a memory I couldn't hold, or imagine, because it was so similar to every other goodbye that I'd had with him. The pain I felt was deep and penetrated every fabric of my being. It was that day that I decided, I never wanted to look death in the eye again.

Unfortunately, it wasn't the first time I'd seen death up close. The first time was a couple of years earlier, in high school. A young man I knew was shot, and I held his hand as he laid by the side of a parking lot, in the grass and mud. His body had become cold and his eyes rolled to the back of his head as I prayed for him, and it was the first time God did not answer my prayer.

When Mary and Martha realized their brother Lazarus was sick, they prayed for him and they sent for Jesus as they knew he could save him. But in order for Jesus to return, he would have to return to the place where people tried to stone him - to kill him.

Horizontal prayer empowers us to trust God in the darkest circumstances, when death seems imminent and when our fears must become courage, and our weakness must become strength.

By the time Jesus arrived, Lazarus was dead for four days. Jesus cried with those who mourned, for he loved Lazarus. But his arrival, his brave journey of thoughtful courage, was not only a necessary milestone in his own life impacting his near future, but it was most importantly to bring glory to God on an eternal landscape. Across the horizon, Jesus knew that he was sent for this moment and those to follow.

Then one of them, named Caiaphas, who was high priest that year, spoke up, "You know nothing at all! You do not realize that it is better for you that one man die for the people than that the whole nation perish."

He did not say this on his own, but as high priest that year he prophesied that Jesus would die for the Jewish nation, and not only for that nation but also for the scattered children of God, to bring them together and make them one. So from that day on they plotted to take his life. (John 11:49-53)

We do not know where God will lead us in this life. We do know that as long as we walk with him, he will lead us on an adventurous path. For Jesus, it led to great sacrifice to the benefit of others, perhaps we will be called upon a similar road of sacrifice for the greater good.

Regardless, horizontal prayers that ask God for a servant's heart, a worshipper's praise, and a will to become the living proof of what a life with Jesus looks like will give us courage, strength, and victory in our time of need.

The Vengeance of the Lord

I hear many whispering, "Terror on every side! Denounce him! Let's denounce him!" All my friends are waiting for me to slip, saying, "Perhaps he will be deceived; then we will prevail over him and take our revenge on him."

But the Lord is with me like a mighty warrior; so my persecutors will stumble and not prevail. They will fail and be thoroughly disgraced; their dishonor will never be forgotten. Lord Almighty, you who examine the righteous and probe the heart and mind, let me see your vengeance on them, for to you I have committed my cause.

Sing to the Lord! Give praise to the Lord! He rescues the life of the needy from the hands of the wicked.

Jeremiah 20:10-13

As a believer, we wish ill will on no one. But there is always a time, a moment when vengeance seems overwhelmingly appropriate. Who better to execute that vengeance, than the Lord Almighty?

When we adopt a lifestyle of praying horizontally, dancing across the landscape of our lives, we see how God has shaped us to become part of Him. We embrace His Will because we can recognize that the determination and strategy of God expands beyond a scope we can imagine or comprehend. The creator of the universe and all

that lives, has lived and will live within it, has a different perspective and objective. Somehow within this grand space, there is a unique place for each of us, individually to do our part, and become all he has ordained us to be.

However, at moments in this process, in embracing this lifestyle of blessing, responsibility, faith, adventure, mercy, and love - as we do what God has called us to do, others may question us. They may taunt us, call us names, or stand in opposition to our thoughts and ideas, or even worse, they may physically assault us in an effort to get rid of us.

There are many examples of this in the Bible, and countless of heroic men and women who stood for what was right in the face of adversity. But it is altogether different when that person is you or I. And this is often, who God has called us to be. The voice of reason in the room, the lone objector in a hallway of mishapen thoughts and subsequent actions, the whistleblower, the plaintiff or the defense. No matter what God has called us to do and or say, we are to do it in spite of those who collectively reject.

This is a strength and courage that only comes from horizontal prayer and thankfully, on the other side of it, God stands as our protector - our mighty warrior.

When God executes his vengeance he leaves no stone unturned, he requites his justice in a way that will allow you to witness that he is in charge and it is he and only he that is sovereign.

As a person who prays horizontally, he has often prepared us to forgive those who hurt us or tried to impede our progress. He insists that we don't become like Jonah, sitting beneath the tree, waiting for God to execute a punishment on those God has every desire to forgive.

God's mercy endures forever. As his children, we must embrace mercy and forgiveness for those who have hurt us most, and let God do what seems right in his heart.

"Vengeance is mine, I will repay." says the Lord. (Romans 12:19)

Do not be deceived: God cannot be mocked. A man reaps what he sows. Whoever sows to please their flesh, from the flesh will reap destruction; whoever sows to please the Spirit, from the Spirit will reap eternal life. (Galatians 6:7-8)

One with God

Sing about a fruitful vineyard: I, the Lord, watch over it; I water it continually. I guard it day and night so that no one may harm it.

Isaiah 27:2b-3

A life with God is more beautiful than we will ever give it credit for. God is with us, in every moment of our lives. In good times and bad times, in hardship, and in joy. He is watching over us to ensure we make it to our intended destination.

On our way, we may experience drought, famine, or fame and success. Either way, God holds the balance, for it is in balance, that God teaches us the value of life over any vanity we may attempt to hold onto.

As we learn to acknowledge Him and hold Him in high esteem, our enemy runs in fear from the power and love that Jesus has for us. Likewise, as we grow with Him, we begin to water those around us with His love and His presence in our lives.

In days to come Jacob will take root, Israel will bud and blossom and fill all the world with fruit. (Isaiah 27:6)

It is through a lifestyle of horizontal prayer that a true life with God begins. For it seems, at least to me, that prior to, we were simply

swimming in shallow water, trying to get to the other side of the pool where salvation awaits.

But as we pray for God to open our eyes in every area of our lives, as we pray for others and our ability to trust beyond our lines of comfort, we experience a revelation. We begin to recognize our finite state of being and appreciate the Lord's ability to not only be here with us in our present, but we can also see God was with us in our past, and we depend on his consistency in our future.

We are grateful and humbled that he is our lifetime companion and the true definition of our existence.

Then we understand that we are not called to play it safe, but to experience the deep and penetrating waves of a tumultuous sea, the danger of life as it calls us to be ambassadors of Christ in a land that often denies that he is Our Savior. When the waves get too high, or the water is seemingly up to our neck, we can stand in faith that the Lord will command those waters to 'be still'.

A New Beginning

It is the Lord your God you must follow, and him you must revere. Keep his commands and obey him; serve him and hold fast to him.

Deuteronomy 13:4

When I imagine looking across a horizon, I see a peaceful ocean view, with the sun rising enveloped by a bright orange sky, and no shore in sight. At other times, I imagine I have the view of an eagle, broad and encompassing, taking in the breathtaking snowcapped mountains and rich valleys below. It is a peaceful vision.

This is beautiful and in my heart and soul, I know that a life, especially an eternal life, with God is beautiful. But in order to maintain the beauty of anything you love, it must remain untainted, unbothered, and function as it was intended to function.

When people enter our lives who do not believe what we believe, they try to persuade us to convert to their beliefs, as we do when they do not believe in Jesus Christ. But if we are in the midst of those who do believe in other religions, it is best not to be exposed or even consider what they have to share. God desires that we are just as committed to him as he is to us.

To entertain other religions is not only a slap in the face to God, but it is also a dangerous path. Consider Balaam in the Bible. He did

not worship God alone, he in fact was well known to speak to many gods, but he also had the unique ability to hear from God. He was often commissioned to work on projects for persons of high authority due to his unique ability to prophesy and speak things into existence (manifestation), and there was a king who asked him to curse the children of God.

> But God said to Balaam, "Do not go with them. You must not put a curse on those people, because they are blessed." (Numbers 22:12)

The king took Balaam to the highest heights in his region and he asked him to look across the horizon. He noted how the children of God were growing in number and would soon become an issue to his reign. Balaam's participation in this activity greatly displeased God. God told Balaam not to go, but he did anyway, because he desired to material gain and power.

God spoke to Balaam again and warned him that not only was he on a dangerous path, but that in fact, his very life was at stake. By following the influence of others, Balaam's confusion could have cost him his life but it would not be at the detriment of God's children. God implicitely told him that he could do nothing but BLESS the children of God. As a result of this ruler's relentless pursuit to destroy the children of God, Balaam instead blessed the children of God seven times.

God is our source, our protection, and our greatest friend. We use horizontal prayer to help us navigate our lives in a way that is pleasing to God, but to also keep us pure to worship God in wholeness and truth. But we must realize that God is also protecting us. When we begin to experience life in this way, it is a new beginning because we have a perception of God's love, a deep and personal relationship with Him that respects and loves him in a way that we would never do anything to hurt him.

Elevation

Everyone brings out the choice wine first and then the cheaper wine after the guests have had too much to drink; but you have saved the best till now.

John 2:10

Life gets better over time. It may not always feel like it though. Growing pains are the worst because it forces you to change when life is already challenging. It can seem that as soon as we get out of the pot that we are tossed into the frying pan.

But we must understand that God is a strategist and he doesn't always let us know the plan.

Jesus was minding his own business, at the wedding with his disciples and mother when suddenly the wedding party ran out of wine. In an instance, he is activated and forced to become what he did not consider himself ready to become.

I can remember when I was a little girl riding on a speedboat with my grandfather and cousin. The boat stopped and we began to coast. Suddenly my cousin picked me up and threw me into the lake. I panicked, I could not swim. He yelled, "Swim! Kick your feets and move your arms!" I was so scared, all I could do was exactly as he instructed. I had on a life jacket and he was there to save me if I failed, but I didn't realize that at the time, all I could do was my best to swim.

Sometimes God will push us right into our destiny. Horizontal prayer prepares us to expect and accept the unexpected - even if our blessing is handed to us on a platter by our enemy, we have to recognize that this is the moment God is going to elevate us!

Just as Jesus answered the moment in obedience to God, we too will do the same.

It Won't Cost You Anything

For this is what the Lord says: "You were sold for nothing, and without money you will be redeemed."

Isaiah 52:3

Most often, when we receive something for free, we might wonder, what is really at stake? But God promised those who choose to believe in Him, that there is no cost for the gift of life he offers.

A life of sin is truly a life of captivity. It's like a prison or a cage that makes you chase what little it gives by way of peace, happiness, joy, and contentment. A life without God is a life that we are tasked to manage on our own. A life of vanity or worship of power, money and material gain is a life that can never bring satisfaction.

For to me, to live is Christ and to die is gain. (Philippians 1:21)

Horizontal prayer comes after submission.

We must submit to God in a way that is not only pure in heart, but also willing to sacrifice the life of sin, self-sufficiency, and gross desire by which we operate in a state of disbelief, dishonesty, and

disdain for the ways of God.

    Our ability to see across the horizon of life comes when we are connected to our compass. God guides us in a way that not only allows us to see today, here, and now but also tomorrow, and an eternity of tomorrows.

    Our acceptance of God allows us to see ourselves. The mirror by which we see ourselves reflects someone that is standing beneath the shadow of the Almighty, one whose strength cannot be overpowered, one whose Word is the final word, one whose presence demands respect and honor, and one who keeps our hearts in the palm of his hand. We see God in us, around us, with us, and within us.

    Horizontal prayer allows us to access the benefits of God for free. Prayer doesn't cost us anything but grants us access to everything. Jesus paid the price so we don't have to. He left us the Holy Spirit that we might experience the greatness of God at no personal cost to us.

    What we give up by way of self-sufficient thinking is far outweighed by what we gain when we simply lay our lives in the hands of our Heavenly Father, and trust Him to guide us day-by-day, step-by-step and moment-by-moment.

    Freedom is the gift that God gives, freedom from sin, self-sufficiency, and an insatiable appetite for more.

The Burden of the Prophet

> But I said, "Alas, Sovereign Lord! The prophets keep telling them, 'You will not see the sword or suffer famine. Indeed, I will give you lasting peace in this place.'"
>
> Then the Lord said to me, "The prophets are prophesying lies in my name. I have not sent them or appointed them or spoken to them. They are prophesying to you false visions, divinations, idolatries and the delusions of their own minds. Therefore this is what the Lord says about the prophets who are prophesying in my name: I did not send them, yet they are saying, 'No sword or famine will touch this land.' Those same prophets will perish by sword and famine.
>
> Jeremiah 14:13-15

As children of God, we are at times, the bearer of unfortunate news. God trusts us to love those he loves enough to tell them the truth despite its dark nature. Our ability to do so, is activated by not only trust of but also by our reverence to God. A Holy God wants those who commit to Him to be Holy as well. When God is sending a message to his people by a prophet, it is a warning of what is to come.

Those affected by the impending doom of God are innocent bystanders, but most often, God warns those who have elected to ignore or deny His existence. In these moments, God will even

Stephanie D. Moore

instruct us on how to respond to their destitute circumstances.

Then the Lord said to me, "Do not pray for the well-being of this people. Although they fast, I will not listen to their cry; though they offer burnt offerings and grain offerings, I will not accept them. Instead, I will destroy them with the sword, famine and plague." (Jeremiah 14:11-12)

    The truth is, when we hear someone crying about their hardships, we want to ease their pain. We want to give them good news, and tell them that God is faithful and that he hears their prayers. While this is true, there are times when God simply tells us that there is a dark season on the way.

    Obedience is a learned trait that takes time, and while we may believe that it should always be our immediate response, it can feel like a burden. But, horizontal prayer helps us to recognize that God is with us in every moment and that he always goes before us to make every crooked place straight. Therefore, our ability to obey his command is reflective of our trust in Him. We can trust that despite how our message is received, we have been ordained to deliver it. We can also trust that regardless of how the intended audience receives our message, God is right there as a witness.

    Anger or danger may result from the person who has the courage to deliver God's message in a timely manner. This is the burden of the prophet, and only through horizontal prayer and consistent communication with God are we able to have the courage to deliver it as God intends. In this we are also equipped to experience whatever may result. And in the end, we still have hope that God will have mercy on all of us.

The Spirit of the Lord

Now the Lord is the Spirit, and where the Spirit of the Lord is, there is freedom.

I Corinthians 3:17

The Old Testament shares the intention of God for us since the beginning of time. To be in relationship with God indicates that we appreciate his presence.

The New Testament addresses what separates us from God. When Jesus died that we may be free from sin, he ripped the barrier that stood between us and God.

As believers of Christ, we are embodied by the Holy Spirit, uniting us with the trinity of God through marriage for eternity.

Today as I watched the news, I saw the story of a teacher who visited Russia and was sentenced to fourteen years in a Russian prison for possession of marijuana. He was freed after three years because he was an American citizen and the President of the United States negotiated for his release. In a similar way, our sins testify against us and are reason for us to be sentenced to death. But because we are in relationship with Jesus Christ, our sins are forgiven. The punishment we deserve is not the punishment we receive. Just as the American's relationship as a US Citizen afforded him freedom, our

relationship with God through Jesus Christ by power of the Holy Spirit affords us the same type of freedom.

In healthy relationships, communication is critical. Effective communication is listening and sharing in a way that is not only meaningful and respectful but it is also filled with a desire for understanding, grace, and the presence of love. This tone of communication, if you will, affords that the desire is not to be right but to gain understanding in a non-threatening way.

When we approach God for vertical prayer, we are often praying for daily direction, protection and provision. When we pray horizontally, we are often praying for an understanding of our purpose, our legacy, and our eternal relationship with Jesus Christ. In each type of communication, we must not only share what is on our hearts with God but we must also be open to hear what God is saying to us as it shapes our behavioral response. We are expressing with sincerity and we are earnestly listening for God's sincere response.

Therefore, to become one with God is to share intimacy with God. In this way, we are free to live an abundant life, filled with the blessings, benefits, and beauty that only a relationship with the Triune God can bring.

The Blessing of Wisdom

My son, do not let wisdom and understanding out of your sight, preserve sound judgment and discretion; they will be life for you, an ornament to grace your neck.

Proverbs 3:5-6

Wisdom is a gift that can save many from undue burden and pain. Wisdom is the bridge between trouble and peace. Wisdom is the patience required to communicate effectively and actively listen. But Godly wisdom is something altogether different.

Godly wisdom allows us access to discernment, it is the Rhema word of God, spoken that we might hear God telling us things that no one else could know. This type of wisdom is only available to those who cherish the intimacy of God. His voice is a small whisper telling us to go, or to stay, or to say what must be said. This is an enormous blessing, the kind of blessing you can't quantify with a number, or justify by any measure, it is the inexplicable exponential blessing of God.

I watched one of those TV shows that share stories of missing people, or those who have been murdered. There was a woman who watched the news and heard the story of a missing girl. When she prayed, she could see the woods and trees. Then on another occasion, she could see a closet. When the police came, they listened

to her. They didn't know why, but they just believed her. When she was asked if she was a psychic, she said, "No, I just pray a lot." Through her relationship with God she was given a vision that no one else could see. Later, they found out that the girl had been murdered and placed into a closet for a long period of time, later the man who murdered her scattered her body in the forest. The police did not find the young lady because of the woman's visions, but when they discovered who murdered her and what happened, her visions aligned with the truth.

Sometimes when we pray, God will reveal what is to come. He will show us visions and signs, other times, we will hear him. Regardless of the way God communicates with us, the fact is, he does and our ability to hear him comes from spending intimate time with God, sitting at his feet and learning from him. It is our desire to be in his presence that allows us to understand the will of God and to receive his Godly wisdom.

By wisdom the Lord laid the earth's foundations, by understanding he set the heavens in place; by his knowledge the watery depths were divided, and the clouds let drop the dew. (Proverbs 3:19-20)

Wisdom is a gift that can open doors that no man can shut. It will place us in the presence of kings when others may see us as paupers. God will reveal his brilliance and allow us access to it, simply because we trust him with our lives and seek his face to aid us at all times.

Lord, you establish peace for us; all that we have accomplished you have done for us.

Isaiah 26:12

Our Heavenly Father is amazing and his love for us is truly immeasurable. His desire to see us walking in grace, favor, and love is evident in the decisions he has made in our best interest. His intentions are pure and what he wants and expects from us is plainly written in the Word of God. The Holy Bible teaches us about the character of God, how he hates evil and he loves a just balance.

This is the definition of peace - to be led by one who loves justice, yet is no respecter of persons, one who is accountable and judges justly.

But for those who despise doing what they should and have malice in their hearts, God has reserved a special justice for them.

But when grace is shown to the wicked, they do not learn righteousness; even in a land of uprightness they go on doing evil and do not regard the majesty of the Lord. Lord, your hand is lifted high, but they do not see it. Let them see your

zeal for your people and be put to shame; let the fire reserved for your enemies consume them. (Isaiah 26:10-12)

There is not a weapon that our enemies can form that will outsmart the desire of God to be good to his people. Even when the enemy feels as though they have won, God shows them that he can see their hearts and their intentions and it will not stand. In this, we can have peace, knowing that God has gone before us to clear danger from our path, and he is behind us watching our back.

The Lord will fight for you; you need only to be still. (Exodus 14:14)

There is something amazing about embracing the peace of God. The peace of God allows you to focus on your purpose and gives you a desire to walk in obedience. Peace provides clarity in moments of confusion and avoids chaos.

In moments of chaos, we are to simply let God fight the battle. This is our gift, our benefit of loving a benevolent God who has a unique zeal to protect his people.

Go, my people, enter your rooms and shut the doors behind you; hide yourselves for a little while until his wrath has passed by. See, the Lord is coming out of his dwelling to punish the people of the earth for their sins. The earth will disclose the blood shed on it; the earth will conceal its slain no longer. (Isaiah 26:20-21)

When trouble pursues us, God instructs us to be still, to wait for him to exact his wrath. For it is God who will avenge us, it is God who protects us, and it is God who sent us.

When we glance across the horizon of our lives, a life we are pleased to live with God at the front, and first in all we do, we see a life of peace that only God can give. This is a peace the world will not understand.

On the Mountaintop

Since then, no prophet has risen in Israel like Moses, whom the Lord knew face to face, who did all those signs and wonders the Lord sent him to do in Egypt—to Pharaoh and to all his officials and to his whole land. For no one has ever shown the mighty power or performed the awesome deeds that Moses did in the sight of all Israel.

Deuteronomy 34:10-12

When you walk with the Lord, God places his fingerprint upon you. There will never be anyone like you, as you will be unique in all your ways. There is simply something special about the person who spends intimate time with God and places Him as a priority in their lives. Exponential gifting and wisdom flow from those who are willing to place God above all else in life. A level of unmistakable discernment is granted to those who seek his face.

Moses prioritized God. He would take time to simply commune with God. This is a trait we see that Jesus also valued, as Jesus also created opportunities to place God first. Moses was a friend of God.

Now Moses used to take a tent and pitch it outside the camp some distance away, calling it the "tent of meeting." Anyone inquiring of the Lord would go to the tent of meeting outside the camp. And

whenever Moses went out to the tent, all the people rose and stood at the entrances to their tents, watching Moses until he entered the tent. As Moses went into the tent, the pillar of cloud would come down and stay at the entrance, while the Lord spoke with Moses. Whenever the people saw the pillar of cloud standing at the entrance to the tent, they all stood and worshiped, each at the entrance to their tent. The Lord would speak to Moses face to face, as one speaks to a friend. Then Moses would return to the camp, but his young aide Joshua son of Nun did not leave the tent. (Exodus 33:7-11)

Moses was entrusted with an immense amount of responsibility.

He was to save his people from slavery and usher his people to the promised land. It was his responsibility to share the Commandments of God with the Israelites, and when their sin grew great, it was his responsibility to stand in the gap and pray for them. He showed them the power of God in his greatness, from the drowning of their enemies in the Red Sea to water flowing from a rock, to manna and quail being delivered from heaven. Moses helped the Israelites understand who God was, he helped them to realize there should be a natural fear of God, and to also believe in the supernatural ability of God.

The mountain top is the summit, it is the furthest and highest place you can go on a mountain.

Our lives are like mountains. The journey can be arduous, discriminating, and even seem impossible. I am certain that Moses faced moments, he could never imagine he would have to face. His purpose demanded he be courageous and say what needed to be said. His purpose demanded his timely response, lest he pay the cost of needless life lost. His purpose demanded a cool and level head, lest he anger God in his quest to please God. His purpose demanded the presence of God in all things he did, that he might reflect the goodness of the Lord.

Moses experienced many incredible things, he watched water turn into blood, frogs upon frogs infest a land, the death angel pass

by, a plague that wiped out most of his people, a man and his family swallowed by the ground, and he even watched as God allowed his goodness to pass him on a mountain. Only Moses could command God and say, "Show me your goodness."

I am certain, Moses felt he was at the top of his mountain every time he experienced something unbelievable, but it was not his season to reach the mountain top, he always had more to do.

As those who pray horizontally, God will give us what may feel as though it is a mountaintop moment - but it will not be. It will simply be another milestone on our way to the summit. We must learn to enjoy our time with God while we are on the way. Just as Moses' trusted God, and was a friend of God, we too must trust him when we cannot trace Him, for surely he is with us.

Beyond

Blessed is the one who does not walk in step with the wicked or stand in the way that sinners take or sit in the company of mockers, but whose delight is in the law of the Lord, and who meditates on his law day and night. That person is like a tree planted by streams of water, which yields its fruit in season and whose leaf does not wither—whatever they do prospers.

Psalm 1:1-3

Green leaves give me excitement as of late, especially those that rest on the plants I water regularly. Just to see life, beaming within each petal, gives me a joy I can't readily describe. The leaves are at times tall, broad, and bravado in character. It's almost as if they are boasting, 'look at me'. The more water and sunlight they receive, the better they off they seem to be. Psalm 1 asserts that when we walk with God, doing his will, adopting his way of life, we are green, full, and like these plants - full of life that everyone can see. God makes everyone around you a witness to the blessing that is on your life. It is not just in the way you carry yourself, but it is also in everything you do. Everything you do will prosper and bring you success. This is God's promise, and it is beyond praying horizontally - it is the blessed life.

Just like any plant, our blessing requires that we stay

connected to our roots. Yes, a leaf disconnected from it's roots cannot receive the life-giving nutrients it requires. Even if you prune a plant with the intention of growing a new one, it will not do so successfully without a good root system connected to it.

> "I am the true vine, and my Father is the gardener. He cuts off every branch in me that bears no fruit, while every branch that does bear fruit he prunes so that it will be even more fruitful. You are already clean because of the word I have spoken to you. Remain in me, as I also remain in you. No branch can bear fruit by itself; it must remain in the vine. Neither can you bear fruit unless you remain in me." (John 15:1-4)

When we find ourselves drowning in life's sorrow, worry, and discontentment, it is a sign - a warning that we may have shifted or drifted from God and a life committed to bring him glory. It may be because we have entered a season of selfishness, or perhaps we experienced a hardship that destroyed our esteem and resolve. Regardless, our pain and desperate plea to gain back what we have lost by any means necessary is a warning that God is not first in our life and we need to return to the vine.

When we are on the vine, we trust God no matter the circumstance. We are broad, bold, and cocky like a tree that is planted by the river yielding fruit in it's season - our leaves don't whither they are prosperous and successful for the world to see. This is the definition of living beyond horizontal prayer.

About the Author

At the age of 9, Stephanie was molested by a friend of my family. In high school, she held the hand of a friend as he died from a fatal gun shot wound... As an adult, she was the victim of a violent acquaintance rape. Subsequently, she struggled with personal demons. But when she sought the Lord and his Word, her life was forever changed.

Give God ALL the Glory!

He is and will always be the head of my life. He is my joy, my strength, my everything.

My constant prayer is to be a perfect conduit of his message and love.

Stephanie was born in Muskogee, Oklahoma. She graduated from Putnam City North High School in 1994. She was married for 16 years. She is the mother of 3 beautiful daughters, and has a grandson named Levi. She graduated with her Associates in Technology, a Bachelor of Arts in Communications, and a Master of Arts in Communication with an emphasis in Political Communication.

She holds several design and technology certifications and has won numerous awards in that area. Stephanie has worked in television, print and web media for more than 16 years.

She is the owner of Moore Marketing and Communications. Her company offers strategic marketing and communication plans, media purchases, public relations, writing services, print services, graphic design and web design. Stephanie has also served as a poltical consultant for Governor, Lt. Governor, State Representative, Mayoral and City Council candidates.

Stephanie has created and sponsored teen etiquette and leadership programs for young ladies and young men. The program for young ladies is called, She's a BOSSE (A Beautiful Oasis of Success, Style and Elegance) and the young man's program is called Grindaholix: Young Men on the Rise.

To date, Stephanie has authored 37 books, 26 of which are daily devotionals. To learn more, visit mooretoread.com.

www.ingramcontent.com/pod-product-compliance
Lightning Source LLC
Chambersburg PA
CBHW071316040426
42444CB00009B/2029